Helping Professions Journal

A Critical Thinking and Reflection Guide

Dianne J. Orton
University of Missouri-Columbia

Fresa J. Jacobs
University of Missouri-Columbia

PEARSON

Boston   New York   San Francisco
Mexico City   Montreal   Toronto   London   Madrid   Munich   Paris
Hong Kong   Singapore   Tokyo   Cape Town   Sydney

Contents

About the Authors

Dianne J. Orton

Dianne Orton has been the Field Practicum Coordinator at the School of Social Work, University of Missouri-Columbia since 1991. Dianne received her Master of Social Work and Master of Arts in Recreation Therapy at the University of Iowa and earned her undergraduate degree in Special Education at the University of Northern Colorado. Dianne's career has included social work positions in the medical, child welfare, and school social work arena. She has also been a special education teacher (K-12) and a higher education administrator in student services at a private institution.

At MU, Dianne is responsible for the management of both the undergraduate and graduate field education programs. She is also an advisor to undergraduate students and teaches field related courses. Dianne's academic interests include: teaching students journal writing techniques during their field practicum experience that emphasis reflection, critical thinking and problem solving skills and visual imagery research which integrates photography and descriptive writing during students' capstone experience.

Fresa J. Jacobs

Fresa Jacobs has worked at the School of Social Work, University of Missouri-Columbia since 1998. She earned a BA in Fine Art emphasis in drawing from the University of Missouri in December of 2000. She also earned a BS in Accounting from Truman State University in May of 1997. Fresa's career has included everything from layout and graphic design to database management and accounts payable. She has played ultimate frisbee in Columbia, MO for the past five years and has organized an ultimate frisbee summer league for the past two years.

Acknowledgments

We would like to thank the numerous undergraduate and graduate social work students at the University of Missouri-Columbia School of Social Work who participated in the journaling activities as part of their practicum assignments. Specifically, we would like to acknowledge the contributions by the following students:

> Becky Beck
> Vicki Davolt
> Kylene Diller
> Chris Kahmke
> Jeanne Link
> Amanda Lohr
> Stephanie Scott
> Alicia Simons
> Dale Smith
> Jennifer Templeton
> Abe Wilks

Introduction

F ield practicums, or internships, are often considered the "heart" of a professional education program. After all the classroom learning, field practicums provide an excellent opportunity for applying that classroom knowledge to a professional setting. This structured learning experience allows for growth both personally and professionally. Hopefully, documenting your field practicum will provide valuable information for reflecting on your experience during and after your practicum.

This journal is a compilation of Structured Activities and Reflections that all interrelate to your practicum. The format is designed around a semester-long practicum but can be easily adapted to other lengths. This journal can be used in an integrative-seminar/capstone experience that is facilitated by field faculty or as an instrument to help increase self-awareness.

Structured Activities: pages 5- 68

Activities are presented in a format that takes you logically from the beginning to the end of your practicum experience. However, there is no rigid format to the order of completion. These activities are meant to challenge you, creating an informal structure for integrating classroom knowledge with professional practice. They require the use of your observation and critical thinking skills.

Roadside Review and Reflection: pages 69- 104

These provide an opportunity to record additional thoughts, ideas and observations in an unstructured manner that assists in self-discovery and professional growth. You may choose not to share these reflections with supervisors and keep them for personal growth and introspection. Sometimes you may struggle with what to write, so here are a few suggestions for jumpstarting your journaling. 1. Review your writings for a Structured Activity for clarification and extending thinking. 2, Respond to a quote or one of the "If You" or "Can You" prompts. Remember, reflections are an opportunity to put your thoughts into cruise control and go with the flow. Recording your reactions and perceptions will empower you to critically evaluate what you are learning.

Content, other than the writing for Structured Activities and Reflections, might include photographs, graphs, sketches, clippings and cartoons. Including copies of your learning plan and evaluation would also be appropriate. Your journal will become a visual and written memoir of your practicum experience. By capturing your experiences you will be able to reread and revisit your journey through your practicum, a story that only you can tell.

First Impressions

You've heard that first impressions are lasting impressions. This concept holds true if you're meeting someone for the first time or visiting an agency for a potential field placement. In either case, that first impression may be difficult to overcome or it may change over time. Whatever the case might be, first impressions are important and need attention.

First impressions involve all your senses, even the way an agency sounds or smells. Take these and other factors into consideration as you begin to describe your first impressions. Once you have recorded your impressions, think about your personal reactions. How do you think a potential client or agency staff would describe the agency?

1st Impressions Example...

What are your initial impressions? Include sights, sounds, smells, office location, office environment, etc.

The smell of the agency is rather bland, with a faint aroma of a sweet flowery smell upon walking in. The air is rather dry inside and tastes like a brisk and cool winter's wind. The first week here was a rather frigid experience, walking into freezer-like temperatures and having to sit in them all day. I learned rather quickly to dress for cool temperatures. Sounds of the agency include the various conversations of the coworkers, both on the phone and in the office (to each other), constant ringing from the phones, clicking from the computer keyboards in the offices, the drawn out, high-pitched squeak from office chairs and the main door, the lone printer spitting out faxes and other sheets, and the occasional blurp, blurp, blurp of the water cooler. As far as the overall feel in the office, there are a number of vents that blow cool air, which creates the "freezer-like temperatures."

How would clients describe the agency?
Recommendations/ Suggestions

If I were a client, or a child aged six to fourteen years old, I would not feel as though the agency was targeted towards me. No toys or kid-friendly posters surround the main common area or conference/interview rooms. Recommendations I would make to create a client-friendly atmosphere include a candy dish, kid posters (with cartoons or new adolescent bands). In addition, pictures of my peers and their "big brothers and sisters" would be neat to see, because upon entrance, aside from the sign with the agency's name, there is no indication of what the organization does.

Your 1st Impressions

What are your initial impressions? Include sights, sounds, smells, office location, office environment, etc.

How would clients describe the agency - what is different?

How would staff describe the agency?

Recommendations/Suggestions

Orientation

A good orientation to the agency is critical for creating a solid foundation for your placement. The orientation process is a collaborative effort between the agency and you, so make sure you actively participate, ask questions.

Feeling prepared to begin your placement helps boost self-confidence. It also helps alleviate some of the initial anxieties about expectations, responsibilities and other concerns. Orientation should include various aspects of the agency and placement such as:

- Supervision expectations
- Placement expectations
- Coworker introductions
- Policy and procedure protocols
- Safety training
- Office equipment
- Learning opportunities

Orientation Example...

Describe your orientation to the agency. Make sure you reference the various aspects of agency and placement orientation.

I was quite impressed with the orientation to the Agency. It was very thorough and informative, making for an excellent introduction to the agency. Prior to the orientation a personal screening was conducted on each of us, involving the normal introductory paperwork, fingerprinting, drug-screening and being photographed for an ID badge. I was a little surprised by the fingerprinting: I'm not sure why that was necessary. Between that and the drug-screening I felt like I was being arrested.

— — — — — — — — — — —

The orientation was awesome! It covered every topic imaginable for such an event, including topics such as: Agency mission, vision and values; boundary issues; fire/safety protocols; abuse and neglect; cultural diversity; suicide awareness; infection control; CPR; confidentiality and privacy, or the Health Insurance Portability and Accountability Act of 1996 (HIPPA); and professional assault response training (PART). The topics that were the most beneficial to me were the safety protocol information and the assault response training.

Your Orientation

Describe your orientation to the agency. Make sure you reference the various aspects of agency and placement orientation.

Did the orientation process answer a majority of your questions, concerns? Why or why not?

Safety

No one is immune from potential involvement in a violent incident, whether it is in your personal life or your field placement. Being prepared is an essential element to reducing the risk of violence. While you cannot eliminate all the potential risk, being aware of the risk and taking preventive measures can help assure safety during the field placement.

Find out the safety measures currently in place within your agency and if the agency provides safety training. Take time to discuss your concerns with your instructors and supervisors. Are there any issues of potential risk and/or safety within the agency that you feel haven't been addressed?

Safetly Example...

What safety guidelines/procedures does the agency have in place to protect staff from potential violent incidents?

I greatly appreciate the thorough training we received; however, now I'm pretty terrified to work with the clients. I knew they were aggressive, but now I feel like assaults are common occurrences. I feel like I'm going to work in a prison rather than a hospital. I'm hoping the clients are not as aggressive as this training made them out to be. Nevertheless, my personal safety plan includes always being aware of my surroundings, paying attention to gut feelings, never putting myself in a situation where I am alone with a client or in a secluded area with a client, and calling for staff support if needed. If I follow this plan, I'm confident I will be safe (for the most part).

Your Safety

What safety guidelines/procedures does the agency have in place to protect staff from potential violent incidents?

What safety training have you received? Has it included instruction in effective communication with clients and techniques for de-escalating hostility and conflict? Did it help alleviate any concerns you have?

What more can you personally do to protect yourself?

Are there any reasons why your agency might be concerned about staff safety?

Learning Plan

One of the first tasks during you field practicum is the development of a learning plan. This plan will help map out practicum tasks, activities, etc. by creating an individualized learning experience. Tailoring the plan to your individual goals and interests, within the context of your degree program and the time span of the practicum, will enhance the learning experience.

The key to a successful learning plan is to make it realistic; your learning plan goals should be attainable and measurable within the time span of your practicum experience. Plans should include tasks that can begin as soon as possible so interest remains high. Taking time to review the learning plan at various stages of the practicum ensures that you are still heading in the right direction. The learning plan should not be a static instrument.

Learning Plan Example...

Goals

1. Increase awareness of mental health issues in physical health setting.
2. Increase competency of interventions in mental health areas
3. Increase knowledge of resources and how to link clients to appropriate resources

Behavioral Objectives

1. Understand how a physical ailment may impact an existing mental health issue and vice versa. Improve communication and knowledge of mental health issues
2. Identify and understand how to determine the impact of mental health issues using social work skills. Sharpen social work skills learned in the classroom.
3. Identify what referrals may be appropriate; thinking beyond the most commonly used resources.

Learning Experiences

1. Observe other social workers who actively aid those with mental health issues. Assist in the ER where domestic violence, rape, abuse and substance abuse are most often present.
2. Seek those clients who have a mental health issues and assess coping and understanding while continually focusing on strengths. Provide education to patients on particular mental illness
3. Research resources both locally and nationally that are available to clients regarding mental health issues. Use NAWS/MASW and the social work database.

Competencies

Supervision and journals. A complete resources list will be completed with other team members.

Your Learning Plan

Goals *should be broad and not specifically measured.*

Behavioral Objectives *are specific and observable activities that help attain Goals.*

Learning Experiences *are tasks, activities that help in achieving Behavioral Objectives and Goals.*

Competencies *are the tools by which you measure goal attainment. Usually include journals, supervision, observation and assessment.*

Trip Timeline

Timelines can help provide a "picture" of your practicum experience. This form of linear diagramming gives a sense of wholeness to the experience, from the first tentative steps to the confident strides.

It will be a challenge deciding what events will best represent your experience. Adding narrative descriptions of experiences will give meaning to events and aid in reflection of your practicum.

Trip Timeline Example...

Jan. 7th – I was pretty nervous my first day because I have never worked with this client population. It looks like I will be sitting in on and participating in several group-style therapies. This will be interesting because I have never done group work – but also a little scary.

Jan 27th – I faced my first challenge within Process Group. A client brought up a subject that was happening in my life at the time and I felt like I could not give feedback without breaking down. I went to my supervisor with these feelings.

Feb 1st – Participated in my first Children's Group, which I really enjoyed. Also, noticed that I was having a hard time holding eye contact during Process Group.

Feb 11th – Came to the realization that not all clients will successfully make it through this program and remain "clean," as one of my favorite clients relapses.

March 3rd – Started creating the curriculum for a new children's group, which will be based on teaching social and behavioral skills.

March 14th – Had the opportunity to participate in a medical assessment screening and clinical assessment.

March 17th – lead my first Process Group with another therapist. I was pretty nervous but it went really well.

March 29th – ran/lead my Process Group all by myself, without a therapist in the room. I had a sticky situation with a new client, who threatened to kill her husband. Went to my supervisor and talked it over, and then we talked w/ client.

April 14th – Lead my last Process Group and said goodbye to the clients. I also said goodbye to all the staff members and gave them each personalized thank you notes. I will miss everyone.

Your Trip Timeline

Identify the milestones of your practicum experience.

Continue your timeline ...

Rules of the Road

L ife is filled with formal and informal rules, practicums are no exception. Learning what these rules are for your agency during you practicum will help determine if your ride is smooth or bumpy. Use all of your senses in your observations because not all rules are verbally communicated.

Rules of the Road Example...

What are some of the informal or formal "rules of the road" at your agency?

Informal - Each department has wardrobe requirements – Social Services is business casual – no denim

Formal - Confidentiality – always watch what you say and where you say it. Guard confidentiality as a precious trust. Respect patient's space and personal needs

It's okay to say what you feel. Respect others with feedback using "I see, I hear, I feel." Do this without criticizing, demeaning or name calling.

Everyone stays until the meeting is done. Respect yourself by staying even when it's not comfortable.

No talking about someone not in group. Respect others by keeping what is said in group – in group.

Patients are expected to adhere to standards that the staff doesn't uphold.

Your Rules of the Road

What are some of the informal or formal "rules of the road" at your agency?

How did you discover these different rules for your agency? What are some of the informal or formal "rules of the road" at your agency?

Rest Stop

Good stress or bad stress, we've all been there at one time or another. Sometime during the practicum you will most likely experience some form of stress. You will probably have a wide variety of emotions, from anxiety to excitement. All of this is occurring while you are juggling studies, work, family, etc. It might be a good time to take a rest stop and enjoy some downtime. Identifying sources of stress can help you in alleviating some stress.

Rest Stop Example...

Were there times you needed to stop, rest, and regroup during your practicum experience?

My sense of running out of time, since I have been in school all my life, I feel like it's time to start enjoying it. Even though this internship is almost over it seems so far away. I've always thought I can do a little more and this time it hit me. It affected my whole life, my physical as well as my mental health. This translated into anxiety, frustration, and anger until my supervisors helped me take charge of the situation and do something about it. My psychological reactions and the exhaustion were shown by my cynicism toward life and less attention to my family when it should have been my first priority. In order to take care of myself until one of my stressors is over I am coming to work later, allowing myself to have time for school projects, taking an hour lunch, and some time off. I also went with a co-worker to a spa for a full body massage to treat myself. It felt so good....

———————————

The situations where I most felt that I need to stop, rest, and regroup are when I am working on linking clients with resources. The reason for this is this is not an easy task. There are many times when getting resources for a client is challenging if not seemingly impossible. Many patients need resources like assistance with transportation, housing, medications, and doctor's fees. It can be very frustrating to make phone calls, fill out mounds of paperwork, and thoroughly question the patient about their income and expenses (which sometimes feels like interrogation to me) and after this long process tell the patient they are not eligible for assistance that is stressful for me. The actual process is busy and sometimes frustrating, but not being able to assist the client in paying for expensive, but needed, services really is hard for me to deal with without stopping and regrouping sometimes.

Your Rest Stop

Were there times you needed to stop, rest, and regroup during your practicum experience? What stressors do you have at work, in your private life and at your practicum?

What are your personal stress indicators and how do you manage them?

What's the difference between "good stress" and "bad stress" for you?

Snapshots

The richness of a practicum experience and its uniqueness can be limited by the traditional forms of communication, writing and verbal reports. An often overlooked channel of communication is the ability to communicate visually. Utilize photography to find a visual and symbolic language for thoughts and abstract concepts. Communicate your perspective of the practicum experience and understand yourself in a professional helping role by incorporating reflective writing with the photograph. This can help you to demonstrate new patterns of thinking to others, make new connections and tell stories about professional practice from your point of view.

Check with your supervisor and be sure to respect confidentiality issues. Take individual photographs of artifacts that reflect your practicum. Now reflect on how each photograph relates to your practicum and your classroom learning, make a copy of worksheet for each photograph.

Snapshots Example...

My Feet - These boots carry me around everyday, to every floor, to every interaction to every patient. These boots are worn down, but they are still hanging in there. At times during the semester I felt overwhelmed and worn down, but I just persevered and have gotten through. These boots are a symbol for being tough and moving on. **Lesson learned:** the importance of perseverance.

- - - - - - - - - - - -

Time - Our practicum required four hundred hours learning about our agency and its services. In order to fulfill this requirement, I must balance my time accordingly. Also, probation and parole is based on time requirements, therefore, part of my learning experience involves knowing those various time stipulations that clients and officers must abide by. We live in a society where time is constant. Learning how to balance time is a task that everyone is faced with. Also, we must be able to organize the importance of our tasks, from most important to least important. Figuring out how to juggle those tasks and manage our time is a skill that P&P officers face. This same skill is expected of our clients on a relative level. Those clients who are good at this skill often are on a less intensive level of supervision and those clients that are not, often are managed on a more intensive level of supervision. In both cases of clients and officers, the better understanding of this skill allows more freedom. **Skill represented:** time management.

Your Snapshots

Adhere your Snapshot here.

What is the title of the photo?

What is the significance of this artifact in relation to your practicum?

Lessons you have learned from this artifact?

Knowledge, values and/or skills this photograph represents?

Ethics

As a helping professional you will be confronted with
ethical problems and dilemmas regarding confidentiality,
boundaries and other related practice and professional issues.
As a student you will make mistakes, learning how to
effectively analyze and resolve them is an important part of
you practicum. Keeping your supervisor informed is critical in
the process.

One of the first steps you should take is to find out what
policies/procedures regarding professional ethics are in place
at your agency. Have you experienced any difficult situations
or ethical dilemmas? Consider how they were resolved, what
did you learn from the situation?

Ethics Example...

Describe a situation during your practicum that resulted in an ethical dilemma.

A student at my placement is the step-daughter of a man arrested for murder. She was heard talking with two other students about having "seen some things" in relation to the murder, as a result the police were contacted and an officer sent to interview the child. I was asked to sit in the initial interview as the school representative.

My dilemma has to do with parent notification and who is responsible for notifying parents. By law, the police can interview a child without an attorney or parent if they are not suspects in the crime. The school didn't notify the parents prior to these interviews. After discussing this situation with the Principal, and two Assistant Principals, we all agreed that since the school is (a) not legally obligated to inform the parents of the interviews (or get permission), and (b) since we provided support for the children (me) which we are not required to do, and (c) due to the fact that the information discovered in the interview was delicate and potentially incriminating, it was best to let the police make the calls to the parents instead of us. In other situations, I would typically call the parent(s) to inform them of the interview. There is no specific policy in these types of situations that clearly states proper procedure.

With all of that said, I would, as a parent, want to be informed if my child was interviewed by anyone without my knowledge. That is why I am struggling with my decision to not call the parent in question. At the same time I believe that there really was no decision to be made by us at school, it was out of our hands. The police department had the authority to do what they did...they are more powerful than us.

Your Ethics

Describe a situation during your practicum that resulted in an ethical dilemma. Who was involved? What ethics (if any) were breached? How was the situation resolved?

What observations could you share with your supervisor regarding ethical conduct or misconduct you have observed at the agency?

Research

Applying research and statistics knowledge in your practicum setting could benefit your practice and assist the agency in evaluating programs and policies. Research efforts can help assure that trust, discretion, performance and quality of services are maintained or improved for the client. Getting started might be a little perplexing but, in conjunction with your supervisor and faculty liaison, you can develop a plan of action that meets your learning needs and agency protocol.

Considering what evaluations are currently in place at your agency, what other areas of service could be evaluated? Are the current efforts adequate?

Research Example...

What research efforts, i.e. evaluations or studies, have your agency conducted, or planned on conducting?

Effective Behavior Strategies (EBS) social skills groups is an ongoing evaluation. EBS is a team of teachers, administrators, and specialists working together to reduce the number of "behavior issues" in our school. Kindergartners through fifth graders are split by grade levels into groups, which are led by the school psychologist, psychology interns, and my field instructor and I. The curriculum calls for puppets, children's literature, posters, and group discussions to be used to teach children appropriate behaviors, such as how to be good listeners, and how to greet adults and peers. Students fill out a self-evaluation at the first and final group meetings, and teachers keep running tallies on how often students in the groups exhibit appropriate behaviors in the regular classroom during a 14-week time period. Group leaders are asked to keep records of each session, and indicate any modifications made to the curriculum.

This type of research could benefit schools with high incidence of "behavioral issues." It would be fascinating to research how poverty, race, and physical/emotional /sexual abuse affect students at different grade levels. It would be extremely beneficial to find out what roles and interventions have been effective or ineffective in schools. Including evaluating various school groups to find out what topics and curricula have the most positive impact in students' lives.

Since obtaining parental consent for field trips is a challenge, we must realize the logistical nightmares with research involving minors. Evaluations and research involving human subjects is always tricky, and must go through the proper channels in order to make sure confidentiality, safety and privacy issues are respected.

Your Research

What research efforts, i.e. evaluations or studies, have your agency conducted, or planned on conducting? How involved was the staff in these efforts?

What changes, if any, have occurred as a result of these findings? How would these findings benefit the agency, clients or staff?

Diversity

W̲e̲ live in a diverse, multi-ethnic society that is changing even as you read this sentence. How you choose to educate yourselves and understand these differences will shape your practicum experience and career as a helping professional. Diversity issues include not only the staff you work with but also the clients or even the board of directors.

Take time to consider how your agency handles diversity issues. How does your own cultural heritage affect these issues?

Diversity Example...

Describe the diversity of staff and/or clients at your agency.

I work with other cultural and racial diversities than my own. I work with African American, as well as Caucasian, children. Learning about their strengths helps me meet the clients where they are, understand where they come from, and how I can best help them develop a positive sense of themselves and find their identity. Learning is an ongoing process; they teach me everyday something new about their music, their codes, and slang. I accept everybody for who they are, not for what they look like. I get along with everybody and if they try to offend me by calling me names, like it has happened before, addressing derogatory names to my race, I do not take it personal. I don't blow up, I don't react, I let them ventilate and when they calm down we process the situation. Actually the child who has called me, mistakenly, a "chink" is the one now that has the best relationship with me. I think being a minority myself has helped me appreciate the beauty in everyone, and instead of concentrating on the differences I concentrate on the similarities we have.

Your Diversity

What barriers, if any, does your agency have in its service delivery to minority populations?

Describe the diversity of clients, staff, board of directors with your agency.

If you could make changes that could benefit minority clients in your agency, what would they be? Policy related? Service delivery related?

How do you think your own cultural heritage affects your work? How would your clients describe your understanding of minority cultures?

Identification

Practicum experience provides the opportunity to apply the knowledge, values and skills you learned in the classroom to the professional setting. By identifying and documenting these abilities you will also be able to transfer them into a resume or portfolio, further illustrating your competence as a helping professional.

Being able to identify an occasion that demonstrates one of these skills can be a bit difficult. Think of the situations that challenged you the most and just start writing because these are usually the areas that were the most beneficial to your professional growth.

Identification Example...

Assessment

It is important to ask clarifying questions, and learn what to ask. I have learned more about the basic steps in an assessment and the importance of picking up and reading verbal and non-verbal messages the clients send. Another important aspect is learning to focus on client strengths and abilities, and not their limitations. I need to be knowledgeable in the different areas (such as cognitive and behavioral abilities), and use that information to focus on the whole person – not on "fixing" a specific problem.

Autonomy / Accountability

"I pump the gas, but the client drives the car." This statement is representative of how we encourage client autonomy. We try to empower the client (or the client's family), without being judgmental of decisions they make. We do not want clients to become dependent on our agency or on services other agencies provide, but to view them as resources to help themselves make their lives better.

Flexibility

I have learned that this is a vital skill for social workers to have. I am a very structured, organized, and scheduled person, which overall is a good thing for a social worker to be. I have found that the schedule I make at the beginning of the day looks very little or nothing like what I actually DO during the day. Clients call with emergencies (crisis intervention), paperwork piles up, and we could net new referrals at any time. Workers have to be flexible in order to deal with these situations, which helps reduce stress and increase organization.

Your Identification

Assessment

Communication

Collaboration/Networking

Resource Development

Case Management

Autonomy/Accountability

Flexibility

Critical Thinking/Problem Solving

Program Evaluation

Other

Inspection

After spending some time at the agency you most likely have some perceptions and opinions to share about your experience. Your experience has probably had many positive and some negative elements. Writing these thoughts down will help you process the experience and should provide you with valuable information regarding your interactions with clients, staff and the agency system.

Inspection Example...

Identify positive and negative aspects of your experience with...

Staff

Staff are very open to helping me learn. They are always there to answer questions and share their experiences. **However,** outside the social services office, I believe some staff truly support our services while others just use them to pass off patients. Sometimes it is as if they do not even try to do things before they call. Also, other professionals don't have the best people skills (i.e. Doctors telling family of patient's condition.)

Clients

Most clients are receptive to a social worker coming in and helping. They seem to be very thankful. **However,** they aren't always appreciative and some try to take advantage of services.

Agency and/or System

The hospital system is very interested in providing quality care and dedicated to teaching. **However,** it is so large it is hard to learn the business side of the agency.

Yourself as a helping professional

I have felt that just being present for patients & their families has been rewarding. I feel that I have learned skills to work better with persons in crisis. **However,** there have been times I have not felt very comfortable with my helping skills – such as when patients die. I never know what to say. I also sometimes have become emotionally attached to certain cases.

Your Inspection

Identify positive and negative aspects of your experience with...

Staff

Clients

Agency and/or System

Yourself as a helping professional

Road Map

Mapping your work with clients can provide information & insight into the effectiveness of your intervention & behavior assessments. It can also be used to gauge your preparedness as a professional helper and fine-tune observational skills.

Field Instructors and students could use the graph that is created to assess the content and feelings experienced during placement in work with individual clients, group sessions, home visits & interdisciplinary team meetings. The vertical axis could be changed and developed as the placement proceeds, becoming more or less complex as the situation warrants. We encourage you to create your own range of feelings, to customize this graph to your needs.

Source: Social Work Practicum I/IA Open Learning Institute, Charles Sturt University

Mapping Example...

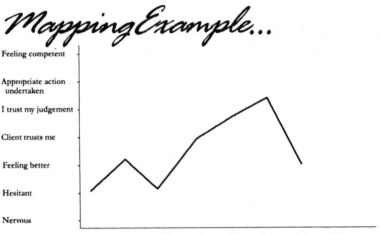

	Feeling competent
	Appropriate action undertaken
	I trust my judgement
	Client trusts me
	Feeling better
	Hesitant
	Nervous

Contacts: 1st 2nd 3rd 4th 5th 6th 7th 8th etc.

C1: Orientation and search for connections. Clients on best behavior, but hesitant with "Getting to Know You" game.

C2: Group is starting to form own identity. Aggressive competitive play, cliquing in activity testing each other and the leader.

C3: Two new members, group is hesitant to let them in. New members on best behavior.

C4: Children are starting to feel ownership of group. Increased connection among members, including new members. Sense of energy. Established group routines, cooperative activity.

C5: Increased mutuality, transference high. Fewer power problems. I feel because children trust me not to put them in harm's way. Group negotiations, Practiced alternative, more adaptive interactive styles.

C6: Children are showing identity of the individual and group. Children get out of their comfort zones by doing role-play effectively.

C7: Closing of group. Regression is apparent. Children seem hesitant to leave and try their newly learned behavioral and social skills in the "real world." Increased passivity. Resurgence of early symptomatology, new dependence on leader.

Your Mapping

Contacts: 1st   2nd   3rd   4th   5th   6th   7th   8th   etc.

Contact 1:

Contact 2:

Contact 3:

Contact 4:

Contact 5:

Contact 6:

Contact 7:

Contact 8:

Destination

Coming to the end of the road and closing the door on this experience will require you to stay focused so you can terminate with clients, staff and supervisors in a professional manner. Some of us are better at saying good-bye and moving on than others. No doubt you are probably preoccupied with graduation, finding a job, graduate school, etc., and you probably have mixed feelings about the ending of your practicum. The feelings of accomplishment in helping clients and completing your education are well deserved.

Putting closure on your experience is an important process. Don't take the backseat approach in this process, be assertive and professional with this ending and see it as a first step in defining yourself as a helping professional. Have you started to think about how you will successfully terminate with clients? Field Instructors? Or Staff?

Destination Example...

Field Instructor – Communicated about my role and function. Outlined my expectations and remained very flexible with my needs to suit my schedule and the agency. Viewed supervision as an honorable professional relationship with an end-date.

Staff – Maintained my time at the agency as a learning opportunity not as an employee. Communicate about after practicum plans and possible job offers. Took from the agency what learning opportunities offered for use in the future.

Clients – I've spent the majority of my time this week preparing myself in wrapping up my internship and saying goodbye to the clients and staff. I felt very honored Tuesday night during the Children's group when the child therapist gave me my own good-bye stone to pass around the group. Each child said goodbye to me and stated one thing that they were going to miss about me. At that time, I realized that I had truly become a part of their group. I then went around and told each child what I would miss about them. As I have told my supervisor several times, I am extremely pleased with how my internship worked out. I walked into this internship a little hesitant, because I didn't think this population was the population I wanted to work with in the future. Not only have I gained a better understanding of this population, but I have also developed a sense of compassion for these women.

Yourself – I left feeling that I had terminated with everyone, but no one terminated with me. Why does this feel like a big deal? Probably because I feel as though I have made some major changes and did my best to learn how my agency operates and it was as if I was never there at all. Oh well, I came, I learned, I experienced, I left a better person.

Your Destination

How are you planning a professional termination with...

Field Instructor

Staff

Clients

Yourself

Thank You's

Expressing your gratitude and appreciation with a thank you note to those people you worked with at the agency is always appreciated. Your supervisor and administrator should receive individual notes, whereas a 'group' thank you to the general staff is appropriate. Try to send the thank you notes out the week after you complete you practicum and before you get busy with other activities. Personalize your thank you notes with a special touch.

Thank You's Example...

Field instructor

Assistance with learning plan.
Providing learning experiences.
Assistance in integrating practice with theory (classroom learning).
Providing supervision and support.
Serving as a mentor/role model.
Consultation on personal growth and development.
Providing constructive feedback.
Commitment on field education.

Agency Administrator

Willingness to participate in field education program.
Providing support for instructors.
Providing office space and access to support staff.

Staff

Providing atmosphere of acceptance.
Inclusion in agency activities.
Providing acceptance as a developing professional and not just a
student.

Your Thank You's

How would you thank those that have helped you along this journey?

Field Instructor

Agency Administrator

Staff

Others

Roadside Review

PASS WITH CARE   **ROUGH ROAD**   **NO U TURN**

Studying the maps, making plans and reviewing progress towards a destination are all components of being prepared. The ride won't be smooth going all the time; there will be bumps, road construction, and detours along the way – that is a guarantee. Your work will often be complex and will seldom be routine. Being an active, engaged learner will keep you in the driver's seat. Reflecting on the events of the week, your actions and reactions can be reviewed for personal and professional growth.

Choose a road sign, or make your own sign, each week that summarizes your experience and write a short overview of your weekly activities. Utilize the reflection space for more in-depth thoughts on the week's learning experiences, for responding to a quote, or responding to one of the "If You" or "Can You" prompts.

Roadside Example...

FUTURE AHEAD — I was preoccupied trying to make decisions about graduate school or job possibilities at graduation.

SHARE THE ROAD — There are three practicum students at my agency. We are all in the same cubicle with one desk, phone and two chairs between us.

NEW SURFACE — I had tons of new learning experiences this week. I ran/lead three groups by myself, and a few situations arose during which I had to be fast on my feet. In my first group there was a new client who started talking about killing her ex-sister-in-law, and the plan as to how she was going to carry this out. This was a completely new situation for me, but I think I handled it pretty well. After group I went to my supervisor to tell her what had happened. She informed me that we are mandatory reporters and that we needed to talk to this client to see if she really had a plan, if she did we would have to report her. After talking to the client my supervisor determined that we wouldn't report her, but I was to write up a No Harm contract and have her sign it. The No Harm contract stated that if at any time this client felt like hurting others, she was to go talk to a staff member.

FULL SPEED AHEAD — This week I was given three cases of my own to case manage. Finally, I don't have to depend on others for work, I can do my own.

Roadside Example...

We build the road and the road builds us.
– Sri Lankan Saying

I don't know how much of the road I'm building, but I can see how the road is building me or maybe it is more like a climb. I'm climbing to a point where I am confident and comfortable with being able to make good decisions, assessments, and judgments. Although this will continue to change as I change jobs and agencies, I think there is a certain place where you can feel good in any situation. The climb is challenging and exciting. I welcome the climb. I'm not discouraged by how far I have to go. I am a little discouraged with the fact that there are many outside distractions slowing the progress of my climb. Even when I'm there, I sometimes think of other things than class work, other business, or personal things. I imagine however that this is only a reflection of what it will be like post graduation, but when I do enter whichever specific field I chose, I hope to have less distractions.

If you & Can you Prompts

If you . . .

1. Were the agency administrator for a day, what would you do?
2. Could make one change that would benefit clients, what would it be?
3. Switched identities with someone in your agency for a day, who would you be, why?
4. Were to prescribe a cure for grief, poverty, human rights, etc. what would it be?
6. Could change the mind of one person, what would you change?
6. Could relive a rewarding experience, what would it be?
7. Could immerse yourself into a different culture, which culture would it be and what would you want to experience?
8. Had to choose one value that represents your beliefs, what would it be?

Can you . . .

1. Describe your first visit to a client's home?
3. Recall a time you co-facilitated a group?
4. Recall an accidental breach of confidentiality?
5. Remember a time you felt unsafe during your internship?
6. Recall a time you felt confident in your social work skills and abilities?
7. Recall a time you needed extra supervision to handle a difficult situation?

Your Roadside Review
For the week of _____
Pick or create a road sign for this week and summarize your experiences.

Your SIgn

Your Reflection

I have always known that at last I would take this road, but yesterday I did not know that it would be today. —Narihara

Your Roadside Review

For the week of _____

Pick or create a road sign for this week and summarize your experiences.

Your SIgn

Your Reflection

All adventures, especially into new territory, are scary. -Sally Ride.

Your Roadside Review

For the week of _____

Pick or create a road sign for this week and summarize your experiences.

Your SIgn	

Your Reflection

In the world there are different and still more different people. Sit and mix with everyone, the way a boat joins the river. -Tulsidas

Your Roadside Review

For the week of _____

Pick or create a road sign for this week and summarize your experiences.

Your SIgn

Your Reflection

Journeyer: one who whirls through other worlds, spinning/spiraling on multidimensional voyages through realms of the wild, which involve quests, adventurous travel, the dispelling of demons, cosmic encounters, participation in paradise. -Mary Daly

Your Roadside Review

For the week of _____

Pick or create a road sign for this week and summarize your experiences.

Your Sign	

Your Reflection

Travel is fatal to prejudice, bigotry and narrow-mindedness.-Mark Twain

Your Roadside Review

For the week of _____

Pick or create a road sign for this week and summarize
your experiences.

Your SIgn

Your Reflection

No matter how far you have gone on a wrong road, turn back. -Turkish proverb

Your Roadside Review

For the week of _____

Pick or create a road sign for this week and summarize your experiences.

Your SIgn

Your Reflection

We build the road and the road builds us. -Sri Lankan saying

Your Roadside Review

For the week of _____

Pick or create a road sign for this week and summarize your experiences.

Your Sign

Your Reflection

One always begins to forgive a place as soon as it's left behind. -Charles Dickens

Your Roadside Review

For the week of _____

Pick or create a road sign for this week and summarize your experiences.

Your SIgn

Your Reflection

It would be nice to travel if you knew where you were going and where you would live at the end—or do we ever know? Do we ever live where we live? Or are we always in other places, lost, like sheep? -Janet Frame

Your Roadside Review

For the week of _____

Pick or create a road sign for this week and summarize your experiences.

Your Sign

Your Reflection

The fear of going too far keeps us from going far enough. -Sam Keen

Your Roadside Review

For the week of _____

Pick or create a road sign for this week and summarize your experiences.

Your Sign

Your Reflection

There are two kinds of travel—first class and with children. -Robert Benchley

Your Roadside Review

For the week of _____

Pick or create a road sign for this week and summarize your experiences.

Your SIgn

Your Reflection

All paths lead to the same goal: to convey to others what we are. And we must pass through solitude and difficulty, isolations and silence, in order to reach forth to the enchanted place... -Pablo Neruda

Your Roadside Review

For the week of _____

Pick or create a road sign for this week and summarize your experiences.

Your Sign

Your Reflection

Mileage craziness is a serious condition that exists in many forms. It can hit unsuspecting travelers while driving cars, motorcycles, riding in planes, crossing the country on bicycles or on foot. The symptoms may lead to obsessively placing more importance on how many miles are traveled than on the real reason for traveling. -Peter Jenkins

Your Roadside Review

For the week of _____

Pick or create a road sign for this week and summarize your experiences.

Your SIgn

Your Reflection

On a long journey, even a straw weighs heavy. -Spanish proverb

Your Roadside Review

For the week of _____

Pick or create a road sign for this week and summarize your experiences.

Your SIgn

Your Reflection

Every land has its own special rhythm, and unless the traveler takes the time to learn the rhythm, he or she will remain an outsider there always.
-Juliette De Baircli Levy

Your Roadside Review

For the week of _____

Pick or create a road sign for this week and summarize your experiences.

Your SIgn

Your Reflection

It is a strange thing to come home. While yet on the journey, you cannot at all realize how strange it will be. -Selma Lagerlof

Additional Notes and Reflections

Additional Notes and Reflections

Additional Notes and Reflections

Additional Notes and Reflections

Additional Notes and Reflections

Additional Notes and Reflections

Additional Notes and Reflections

Additional Notes and Reflections

Additional Notes and Reflections

Additional Notes and Reflections

Additional Notes and Reflections

Additional Notes and Reflections

Additional Notes and Reflections

Additional Notes and Reflections

Additional Notes and Reflections

Additional Notes and Reflections

Additional Notes and Reflections

Additional Notes and Reflections